JOHN DRYDEN

ABSALOM & ACHITOPHEL

Absalom and Achitophel (1682)
John Dryden (1631-1700)

ISBN-13:
978-1517479855

ISBN-10:
1517479851

Contents

To the Reader. 5

Part I. 9

Part II. 45

A Key to Both Parts of Absalom and Achitophel. 87

TO THE READER.

It is not my intention to make an apology for my poem: some will think it needs no excuse, and others will receive none. The design I am sure is honest: but he who draws his pen for one party, must expect to make enemies of the other. For wit and fool are consequence of Whig and Tory; and every man is a knave or an ass to the contrary side. There is a treasury of merits in the Fanatic church, as well as in the Popish; and a pennyworth to be had of saintship, honesty, and poetry, for the lewd, the factious, and the blockheads: but the longest chapter in Deuteronomy has not curses enough for an Anti-Bromingham. My comfort is, their manifest prejudice to my cause will render their judgment of less authority against me. Yet if a poem have genius, it will force its own reception in the world. For there is a sweetness in good verse, which tickles even while it hurts; and no man can be heartily angry with him who pleases him against his will. The commendation of adversaries is the greatest triumph of a writer, because it never comes unless extorted. But I can be satisfied on more easy terms: if I happen to please the more moderate sort, I shall be sure of an honest party, and, in all probability, of the best judges; for the least concerned are commonly the least corrupt. And I confess I have laid in for those, by rebating the satire (where justice would allow it), from carrying too sharp an edge. They who can criticise so weakly as to imagine I have done my worst, may be convinced, at their own cost, that I can write severely, with more ease than I can gently. I have but laughed at some men's follies, when I could have declaimed against their vices; and other men's virtues I have commended, as freely as I have taxed their crimes. And now, if you are a malicious reader, I expect you should return upon me that I affect to be thought more impartial than I am. But if men are not to be judged by their professions, God forgive you Commonwealth's-men for professing so plausibly for the government. You cannot be so unconscionable as to charge me for not subscribing my name; for that would reflect too grossly upon your own party, who never dare, though they have the advantage of a jury to secure them. If you like not my poem, the fault may possibly be in my writing (though it is hard for an author to judge against himself); but more probably it is in your morals, which cannot bear the truth of it. The violent on both sides will condemn the character of Absalom, as either too favourably or too hardly drawn. But they are not the violent whom I desire to please. The fault on the right hand is to extenuate, palliate, and indulge; and to confess freely, I have endeavoured to commit it. Besides the respect which I owe his birth, I have a greater for his heroic virtues; and David himself could not be more tender of the young man's life, than I would be of his reputation. But since the most excellent natures are always the most easy, and, as being such, are the soonest perverted by ill counsels, especially when baited with fame and glory; it is no more a wonder that he withstood not the temptations of Achitophel, than it was for Adam not to have resisted the two devils, the serpent and the woman. The conclusion of the story I purposely forbore to prosecute, because I could not obtain from myself to show Absalom unfortunate. The frame of it was cut out but for a picture to the waist; and if the draught be so far true, it is as much as I designed.

Were I the inventor, who am only the historian, I should certainly conclude the piece with the reconcilement of Absalom to David. And who knows but this may come to pass? Things were not brought to an extremity where I left the story: there seems yet to be room left for a composure; hereafter there may be only for pity. I have not so much as an uncharitable wish against Achitophel, but am content to be accused of a good-natured error, and to hope with Origen, that the devil himself may at last be saved. For which reason, in this poem, he is neither brought to set his house in order, nor to dispose of his person afterwards as he in wisdom shall think fit. God is infinitely merciful; and his vicegerent is only not so, because he is not infinite.

The true end of satire is the amendment of vices by correction. And he who writes honestly is no more an enemy to the offender, than the physician to the patient, when he prescribes harsh remedies to an inveterate disease; for those are only in order to prevent the chirurgeon's work of an *Ense rescindendum*, which I wish not to my very enemies. To conclude all; if the body politic have any analogy to the natural, in my weak judgment, an act of oblivion were as necessary in a hot distempered state, as an opiate would be in a raging fever.

PART I.

— Si propiùs stes
Te capiet magis —

In pious times, ere priestcraft did begin,
Before polygamy was made a sin;
When man on many multiplied his kind,
Ere one to one was cursedly confined;
When nature prompted, and no law denied
Promiscuous use of concubine and bride;
Then Israel's monarch after Heaven's own heart,
His vigorous warmth did variously impart
To wives and slaves; and wide as his command,
Scatter'd his Maker's image through the land. 10
Michal, of royal blood, the crown did wear;
A soil ungrateful to the tiller's care:
Not so the rest; for several mothers bore
To god-like David several sons before.
But since like slaves his bed they did ascend,
No true succession could their seed attend.
Of all the numerous progeny was none
So beautiful, so brave, as Absalom:
Whether inspired by some diviner lust,
His father got him with a greater gust; 20
Or that his conscious destiny made way,
By manly beauty to imperial sway.
Early in foreign fields he won renown,

With kings and states allied to Israel's crown:
In peace the thoughts of war he could remove,
And seem'd as he were only born for love.
Whate'er he did, was done with so much ease,
In him alone 'twas natural to please:
His motions all accompanied with grace;
And Paradise was open'd in his face. 30
With secret joy indulgent David view'd
His youthful image in his son renew'd:
To all his wishes nothing he denied;
And made the charming Annabell[1] his bride.
What faults he had (for who from faults is free?)
His father could not, or he would not see.
Some warm excesses which the law forbore,
Were construed youth that purged by boiling o'er;
And Amnon's murder by a specious name,
Was call'd a just revenge for injured fame. 40
Thus praised and loved, the noble youth remain'd,
While David undisturb'd in Sion reign'd.
But life can never be sincerely blest:
Heaven punishes the bad, and proves the best.
The Jews, a headstrong, moody, murmuring race,
As ever tried the extent and stretch of grace;
God's pamper'd people, whom, debauch'd with ease,
No king could govern, nor no god could please;
(Gods they had tried of every shape and size,
That god-smiths could produce, or priests devise): 50
These Adam-wits,[2] too fortunately free,

---

1. 'Annabel:' Lady Ann Scott, daughter of Francis, third Earl of Buccleuch.
2. 'Adam-wits:' comparing the discontented to Adam and his fall.

Began to dream they wanted liberty;
And when no rule, no precedent was found,
Of men by laws less circumscribed and bound;
They led their wild desires to woods and caves,
And thought that all but savages were slaves.
They who, when Saul was dead, without a blow,
Made foolish Ishbosheth the crown forego;
Who banish'd David did from Hebron bring,
And with a general shout proclaim'd him king: 60
Those very Jews, who, at their very best,
Their humour more than loyalty express'd,
Now wonder'd why so long they had obey'd
An idol monarch, which their hands had made;
Thought they might ruin him they could create,
Or melt him to that golden calf — a state.
But these were random bolts: no form'd design,
Nor interest made the factious crowd to join:
The sober part of Israel, free from stain,
Well knew the value of a peaceful reign; 70
And, looking backward with a wise affright,
Saw seams of wounds dishonest to the sight:
In contemplation of whose ugly scars,
They cursed the memory of civil wars.
The moderate sort of men thus qualified,
Inclined the balance to the better side;
And David's mildness managed it so well,
The bad found no occasion to rebel.
But when to sin our biass'd nature leans,
The careful devil is still at hand with means; 80

And providently pimps for ill desires:
The good old cause revived a plot requires.
Plots, true or false, are necessary things,
To raise up commonwealths, and ruin kings.
 The inhabitants of old Jerusalem
Were Jebusites; the town so call'd from them;
And theirs the native right —
But when the chosen people grew more strong,
The rightful cause at length became the wrong;
And every loss the men of Jebus bore, 90
They still were thought God's enemies the more.
Thus worn or weaken'd, well or ill content,
Submit they must to David's government:
Impoverish'd and deprived of all command,
Their taxes doubled as they lost their land;
And, what was harder yet to flesh and blood,
Their gods disgraced, and burnt like common wood.
This set the heathen priesthood in a flame;
For priests of all religions are the same.
Of whatsoe'er descent their godhead be, 100
Stock, stone, or other homely pedigree,
In his defence his servants are as bold,
As if he had been born of beaten gold.
The Jewish rabbins, though their enemies,
In this conclude them honest men and wise:
For 'twas their duty, all the learned think,
To espouse his cause by whom they eat and drink.
From hence began that Plot, the nation's curse,
Bad in itself, but represented worse;

Raised in extremes, and in extremes decried: 110
With oaths affirm'd, with dying vows denied;
Not weigh'd nor winnow'd by the multitude;
But swallow'd in the mass, unchew'd and crude.
Some truth there was, but dash'd and brew'd with lies,
To please the fools, and puzzle all the wise.
Succeeding times did equal folly call,
Believing nothing, or believing all.
The Egyptian rites the Jebusites embraced,
Where gods were recommended by their taste.
Such savoury deities must needs be good, 120
As served at once for worship and for food.
By force they could not introduce these gods;
For ten to one in former days was odds.
So fraud was used, the sacrificer's trade:
Fools are more hard to conquer than persuade.
Their busy teachers mingled with the Jews,
And raked for converts even the court and stews:
Which Hebrew priests the more unkindly took,
Because the fleece accompanies the flock,
Some thought they God's anointed meant to slay 130
By guns, invented since full many a day:
Our author swears it not; but who can know
How far the devil and Jebusites may go?
This Plot, which fail'd for want of common sense,
Had yet a deep and dangerous consequence:
For as, when raging fevers boil the blood,
The standing lake soon floats into a flood,
And every hostile humour, which before

Slept quiet in its channels, bubbles o'er;
So several factions from this first ferment, 140
Work up to foam, and threat the government.
Some by their friends, more by themselves thought wise,
Opposed the power to which they could not rise.
Some had in courts been great, and, thrown from thence,
Like fiends were harden'd in impenitence.
Some, by their monarch's fatal mercy, grown,
From pardon'd rebels, kinsmen to the throne,
Were raised in power and public office high;
Strong bands, if bands ungrateful men could tie.
  Of these, the false Achitophel was first; 150
A name to all succeeding ages cursed:
For close designs, and crooked counsels fit;
Sagacious, bold, and turbulent of wit;
Restless, unfix'd in principles and place;
In power unpleased, impatient of disgrace:
A fiery soul, which, working out its way,
Fretted the pigmy body to decay,
And o'er-inform'd the tenement of clay.
A daring pilot in extremity;
Pleased with the danger, when the waves went high, 160
He sought the storms; but for a calm unfit,
Would steer too nigh the sands, to boast his wit.
Great wits are sure to madness near allied,
And thin partitions do their bounds divide;
Else why should he, with wealth and honour blest,
Refuse his age the needful hours of rest?
Punish a body which he could not please;

Bankrupt of life, yet prodigal of ease?
And all to leave what with his toil he won,
To that unfeather'd two-legg'd thing, a son; 170
Got, while his soul did huddled notions try;
And born a shapeless lump, like anarchy.
In friendship false, implacable in hate;
Resolved to ruin, or to rule the state.
To compass this, the triple bond* he broke;
The pillars of the public safety shook;
And fitted Israel for a foreign yoke:
Then seized with fear, yet still affecting fame,
Usurp'd a patriot's all-atoning name.
So easy still it proves, in factious times, 180
With public zeal to cancel private crimes!
How safe is treason, and how sacred ill,
Where none can sin against the people's will!
Where crowds can wink, and no offence be known,
Since in another's guilt they find their own!
Yet fame deserved no enemy can grudge;
The statesman we abhor, but praise the judge.
In Israel's courts ne'er sat an Abethdin
With more discerning eyes, or hands more clean,
Unbribed, unsought, the wretched to redress; 190
Swift of despatch, and easy of access.
Oh! had he been content to serve the crown,
With virtues only proper to the gown;
Or had the rankness of the soil been freed
From cockle, that oppress'd the noble seed;

---

* 'Triple bond:' alliance between England, Sweden, and Holland; broken by the second Dutch war through the influence of France and Shaftesbury.

David for him his tuneful harp had strung,
And Heaven had wanted one immortal song.
But wild ambition loves to slide, not stand,
And fortune's ice prefers to virtue's land.
Achitophel, grown weary to possess 200
A lawful fame, and lazy happiness,
Disdain'd the golden fruit to gather free,
And lent the crowd his arm to shake the tree.
Now, manifest of crimes contrived long since,
He stood at bold defiance with his prince;
Held up the buckler of the people's cause
Against the crown, and skulk'd behind the laws.
The wish'd occasion of the plot he takes;
Some circumstances finds, but more he makes;
By buzzing emissaries fills the ears 210
Of listening crowds with jealousies and fears
Of arbitrary counsels brought to light,
And proves the king himself a Jebusite.
Weak arguments! which yet he knew full well
Were strong with people easy to rebel.
For, govern'd by the moon, the giddy Jews
Tread the same track, when she the prime renews;
And once in twenty years, their scribes record,
By natural instinct they change their lord.
Achitophel still wants a chief, and none 220
Was found so fit as warlike Absalom.
Not that he wish'd his greatness to create,
For politicians neither love nor hate:
But, for he knew his title not allow'd,

Would keep him still depending on the crowd:
That kingly power, thus ebbing out, might be
Drawn to the dregs of a democracy.
Him he attempts with studied arts to please,
And sheds his venom in such words as these:
  Auspicious prince! at whose nativity 230
Some royal planet ruled the southern sky;
Thy longing country's darling and desire;
Their cloudy pillar and their guardian fire:
Their second Moses, whose extended wand
Divides the seas, and shows the promised land:
Whose dawning day, in every distant age,
Has exercised the sacred prophet's rage:
The people's prayer, the glad diviner's theme,
The young men's vision, and the old men's dream!
Thee, Saviour, thee the nation's vows confess, 240
And, never satisfied with seeing, bless:
Swift, unbespoken pomps thy steps proclaim,
And stammering babes are taught to lisp thy name.
How long wilt thou the general joy detain,
Starve and defraud the people of thy reign!
Content ingloriously to pass thy days,
Like one of virtue's fools that feed on praise;
Till thy fresh glories, which now shine so bright,
Grow stale, and tarnish with our daily sight?
Believe me, royal youth, thy fruit must be 250
Or gather'd ripe, or rot upon the tree.
Heaven has to all allotted, soon or late,
Some lucky revolution of their fate:

Whose motions, if we watch and guide with skill,
(For human good depends on human will,)
Our fortune rolls as from a smooth descent,
And from the first impression takes the bent:
But if, unseized, she glides away like wind,
And leaves repenting folly far behind.
Now, now she meets you with a glorious prize, 260
And spreads her locks before her as she flies.
Had thus old David, from whose loins you spring,
Not dared when fortune called him to be king,
At Gath an exile he might still remain,
And Heaven's anointing oil had been in vain.
Let his successful youth your hopes engage;
But shun the example of declining age:
Behold him setting in his western skies,
The shadows lengthening as the vapours rise.
He is not now, as when on Jordan's sand 270
The joyful people throng'd to see him land,
Covering the beach and blackening all the strand;
But, like the prince of angels, from his height
Comes tumbling downward with diminish'd light:
Betray'd by one poor Plot to public scorn:
(Our only blessing since his cursed return:)
Those heaps of people which one sheaf did bind,
Blown off and scatter'd by a puff of wind.
What strength can he to your designs oppose,
Naked of friends, and round beset with foes? 280
If Pharaoh's doubtful succour he should use,
A foreign aid would more incense the Jews:

Proud Egypt would dissembled friendship bring;
Foment the war, but not support the king:
Nor would the royal party e'er unite
With Pharaoh's arms to assist the Jebusite;
Or if they should, their interest soon would break,
And with such odious aid make David weak.
All sorts of men, by my successful arts,
Abhorring kings, estrange their alter'd hearts 290
From David's rule: and 'tis their general cry —
Religion, commonwealth, and liberty.
If you, as champion of the public good,
Add to their arms a chief of royal blood,
What may not Israel hope, and what applause
Might such a general gain by such a cause?
Not barren praise alone — that gaudy flower,
Fair only to the sight — but solid power:
And nobler is a limited command,
Given by the love of all your native land, 300
Than a successive title, long and dark,
Drawn from the mouldy rolls of Noah's ark.
  What cannot praise effect in mighty minds,
When flattery soothes, and when ambition blinds?
Desire of power, on earth a vicious weed,
Yet sprung from high, is of celestial seed:
In God 'tis glory; and when men aspire,
'Tis but a spark too much of heavenly fire.
The ambitious youth, too covetous of fame,
Too full of angels' metal in his frame, 310
Unwarily was led from virtue's ways,

Made drunk with honour, and debauch'd with praise.
Half loath, and half consenting to the ill,
For royal blood within him struggled still,
He thus replied:— And what pretence have I
To take up arms for public liberty?
My father governs with unquestion'd right,
The faith's defender, and mankind's delight;
Good, gracious, just, observant of the laws;
And Heaven by wonders has espoused his cause. 320
Whom has he wrong'd, in all his peaceful reign?
Who sues for justice to his throne in vain?
What millions has he pardon'd of his foes,
Whom just revenge did to his wrath expose!
Mild, easy, humble, studious of our good;
Inclined to mercy, and averse from blood.
If mildness ill with stubborn Israel suit,
His crime is God's beloved attribute.
What could he gain his people to betray,
Or change his right for arbitrary sway? 330
Let haughty Pharaoh curse with such a reign
His fruitful Nile, and yoke a servile train.
If David's rule Jerusalem displease,
The dog-star heats their brains to this disease.
Why then should I, encouraging the bad,
Turn rebel and run popularly mad?
Were he a tyrant, who by lawless might
Oppress'd the Jews, and raised the Jebusite,
Well might I mourn; but nature's holy bands
Would curb my spirits, and restrain my hands: 340

The people might assert their liberty;
But what was right in them were crime in me.
His favour leaves me nothing to require,
Prevents my wishes, and outruns desire.
What more can I expect while David lives?
All but his kingly diadem he gives:
And that — But here he paused; then, sighing, said —
Is justly destined for a worthier head.
For when my father from his toils shall rest,
And late augment the number of the blest, 350
His lawful issue shall the throne ascend,
Or the collateral line, where that shall end.
His brother, though oppress'd with vulgar spite,
Yet dauntless, and secure of native right,
Of every royal virtue stands possess'd;
Still dear to all the bravest and the best.
His courage foes — his friends his truth proclaim;
His loyalty the king — the world his fame.
His mercy even the offending crowd will find;
For sure he comes of a forgiving kind. 360
Why should I then repine at Heaven's decree,
Which gives me no pretence to royalty?
Yet, oh! that fate, propitiously inclined,
Had raised my birth, or had debased my mind;
To my large soul not all her treasure lent,
And then betray'd it to a mean descent!
I find, I find my mounting spirits bold,
And David's part disdains my mother's mould.
Why am I scanted by a niggard birth?

My soul disclaims the kindred of her earth; 370
And, made for empire, whispers me within,
Desire of greatness is a god-like sin.
  Him staggering so, when hell's dire agent found,
While fainting virtue scarce maintain'd her ground,
He pours fresh forces in, and thus replies:
  The eternal God, supremely good and wise,
Imparts not these prodigious gifts in vain;
What wonders are reserved to bless your reign!
Against your will your arguments have shown,
Such virtue's only given to guide a throne. 380
Not that your father's mildness I contemn;
But manly force becomes the diadem.
'Tis true he grants the people all they crave;
And more perhaps than subjects ought to have:
For lavish grants suppose a monarch tame,
And more his goodness than his wit proclaim.
But when should people strive their bonds to break,
If not when kings are negligent or weak?
Let him give on till he can give no more,
The thrifty Sanhedrim shall keep him poor; 390
And every shekel which he can receive,
Shall cost a limb of his prerogative.
To ply him with new plots shall be my care;
Or plunge him deep in some expensive war;
Which, when his treasure can no more supply,
He must with the remains of kingship buy
His faithful friends, our jealousies and fears
Call Jebusites, and Pharaoh's pensioners;

Whom when our fury from his aid has torn,
He shall be naked left to public scorn. 400
The next successor, whom I fear and hate,
My arts have made obnoxious to the state;
Turn'd all his virtues to his overthrow,
And gain'd our elders to pronounce a foe.
His right, for sums of necessary gold,
Shall first be pawn'd, and afterwards be sold;
Till time shall ever-wanting David draw,
To pass your doubtful title into law;
If not, the people have a right supreme
To make their kings, for kings are made for them. 410
All empire is no more than power in trust,
Which, when resumed, can be no longer just.
Succession, for the general good design'd,
In its own wrong a nation cannot bind:
If altering that the people can relieve,
Better one suffer than a nation grieve.
The Jews well know their power: ere Saul they chose,
God was their king, and God they durst depose.
Urge now your piety, your filial name,
A father's right, and fear of future fame; 420
The public good, that universal call,
To which even Heaven submitted, answers all.
Nor let his love enchant your generous mind;
'Tis nature's trick to propagate her kind.
Our fond begetters, who would never die,
Love but themselves in their posterity.
Or let his kindness by the effects be tried,

Or let him lay his vain pretence aside.
God said, he loved your father; could he bring
A better proof, than to anoint him king? 430
It surely show'd he loved the shepherd well,
Who gave so fair a flock as Israel.
Would David have you thought his darling son?
What means he then to alienate the crown?
The name of godly he may blush to bear:
Is't after God's own heart to cheat his heir?
He to his brother gives supreme command,
To you a legacy of barren land;
Perhaps the old harp, on which he thrums his lays,
Or some dull Hebrew ballad in your praise. 440
Then the next heir, a prince severe and wise,
Already looks on you with jealous eyes;
Sees through the thin disguises of your arts,
And marks your progress in the people's hearts;
Though now his mighty soul its grief contains:
He meditates revenge who least complains;
And like a lion, slumbering in the way,
Or sleep dissembling, while he waits his prey,
His fearless foes within his distance draws,
Constrains his roaring, and contracts his paws; 450
Till at the last his time for fury found,
He shoots with sudden vengeance from the ground;
The prostrate vulgar passes o'er and spares,
But with a lordly rage his hunters tears.
Your case no tame expedients will afford:
Resolve on death, or conquest by the sword,

Which for no less a stake than life you draw;
And self-defence is nature's eldest law.
Leave the warm people no considering time:
For then rebellion may be thought a crime. 460
Avail yourself of what occasion gives,
But try your title while your father lives:
And that your arms may have a fair pretence,
Proclaim you take them in the king's defence;
Whose sacred life each minute would expose
To plots, from seeming friends, and secret foes.
And who can sound the depth of David's soul?
Perhaps his fear, his kindness may control.
He fears his brother, though he loves his son,
For plighted vows too late to be undone. 470
If so, by force he wishes to be gain'd:
By women's lechery to seem constrain'd.
Doubt not; but, when he most affects the frown,
Commit a pleasing rape upon the crown.
Secure his person to secure your cause:
They who possess the prince possess the laws.
 He said, and this advice above the rest,
With Absalom's mild nature suited best;
Unblamed of life, ambition set aside,
Not stain'd with cruelty, nor puff'd with pride, 480
How happy had he been, if destiny
Had higher placed his birth, or not so high!
His kingly virtues might have claim'd a throne,
And bless'd all other countries but his own.
But charming greatness since so few refuse,

'Tis juster to lament him than accuse.
Strong were his hopes a rival to remove,
With blandishments to gain the public love:
To head the faction while their zeal was hot,
And popularly prosecute the Plot. 490
To further this, Achitophel unites
The malcontents of all the Israelites:
Whose differing parties he could wisely join,
For several ends to serve the same design.
The best — and of the princes some were such —
Who thought the power of monarchy too much;
Mistaken men, and patriots in their hearts;
Not wicked, but seduced by impious arts.
By these the springs of property were bent,
And wound so high, they crack'd the government. 500
The next for interest sought to embroil the state,
To sell their duty at a dearer rate,
And make their Jewish markets of the throne;
Pretending public good, to serve their own.
Others thought kings an useless heavy load,
Who cost too much, and did too little good.
These were for laying honest David by,
On principles of pure good husbandry.
With them join'd all the haranguers of the throng,
That thought to get preferment by the tongue. 510
Who follow next a double danger bring,
Not only hating David, but the king;
The Solyimaean rout; well versed of old
In godly faction, and in treason bold;

Cowering and quaking at a conqueror's sword,
But lofty to a lawful prince restored;
Saw with disdain an Ethnic plot begun,
And scorn'd by Jebusites to be outdone.
Hot Levites headed these; who pull'd before
From the ark, which in the Judges' days they bore, 520
Resumed their cant, and with a zealous cry,
Pursued their old beloved theocracy:
Where Sanhedrim and priest enslaved the nation,
And justified their spoils by inspiration:
For who so fit to reign as Aaron's race,
If once dominion they could found in grace?
These led the pack; though not of surest scent,
Yet deepest mouth'd against the government.
A numerous host of dreaming saints succeed,
Of the true old enthusiastic breed: 530
'Gainst form and order they their power employ,
Nothing to build, and all things to destroy.
But far more numerous was the herd of such,
Who think too little, and who talk too much.
These out of mere instinct, they knew not why,
Adored their fathers' God and property;
And by the same blind benefit of fate,
The Devil and the Jebusite did hate:
Born to be saved, even in their own despite,
Because they could not help believing right. 540
  Such were the tools: but a whole Hydra more
Remains of sprouting heads too long to score.
Some of their chiefs were princes of the land:

In the first rank of these did Zimri stand;
A man so various, that he seem'd to be
Not one, but all mankind's epitome:
Stiff in opinions, always in the wrong;
Was everything by starts, and nothing long;
But, in the course of one revolving moon,
Was chemist, fiddler, statesman, and buffoon: 550
Then all for women, painting, rhyming, drinking,
Besides ten thousand freaks that died in thinking.
Blest madman, who could every hour employ,
With something new to wish, or to enjoy!
Railing and praising were his usual themes;
And both, to show his judgment, in extremes:
So over violent, or over civil,
That every man with him was God or Devil.
In squandering wealth was his peculiar art:
Nothing went unrewarded but desert. 560
Beggar'd by fools, whom still he found too late;
He had his jest, and they had his estate.
He laugh'd himself from court; then sought relief
By forming parties, but could ne'er be chief:
For, spite of him the weight of business fell
On Absalom and wise Achitophel:
Thus, wicked but in will, of means bereft,
He left not faction, but of that was left.
  Titles and names 'twere tedious to rehearse
Of lords, below the dignity of verse. 570
Wits, warriors, commonwealth's-men, were the best:
Kind husbands, and mere nobles, all the rest.

And therefore, in the name of dulness, be
The well-hung Balaam and cold Caleb free:
And canting Nadab let oblivion damn,
Who made new porridge for the paschal lamb.
Let friendship's holy band some names assure;
Some their own worth, and some let scorn secure.
Nor shall the rascal rabble here have place,
Whom kings no titles gave, and God no grace: 580
Not bull-faced Jonas, who could statutes draw
To mean rebellion, and make treason law.
But he, though bad, is follow'd by a worse,
The wretch who Heaven's anointed dared to curse;
Shimei, whose youth did early promise bring
Of zeal to God and hatred to his king,
Did wisely from expensive sins refrain,
And never broke the Sabbath but for gain;
Nor ever was he known an oath to vent,
Or curse, unless against the government. 590
Thus heaping wealth by the most ready way
Among the Jews, which was to cheat and pray;
The city, to reward his pious hate
Against his master, chose him magistrate.
His hand a vare* of justice did uphold;
His neck was loaded with a chain of gold.
During his office treason was no crime;
The sons of Belial had a glorious time:
For Shimei, though not prodigal of pelf,
Yet loved his wicked neighbour as himself. 600

---

* 'Vare:' *i.e.*, wand, from Spanish *vara*.

When two or three were gather'd to declaim
Against the monarch of Jerusalem,
Shimei was always in the midst of them;
And if they cursed the king when he was by,
Would rather curse than break good company.
If any durst his factious friends accuse,
He pack'd a jury of dissenting Jews;
Whose fellow-feeling in the godly cause
Would free the suffering saint from human laws.
For laws are only made to punish those 610
Who serve the king, and to protect his foes.
If any leisure time he had from power
(Because 'tis sin to misemploy an hour),
His business was, by writing to persuade,
That kings were useless and a clog to trade;
And, that his noble style he might refine,
No Rechabite more shunn'd the fumes of wind.
Chaste were his cellars, and his shrivel board
The grossness of a city feast abhorr'd;
His cooks with long disuse their trade forgot; 620
Cool was his kitchen, though his brains were hot.
Such frugal virtue malice may accuse,
But sure 'twas necessary to the Jews;
For towns, once burnt, such magistrates require
As dare not tempt God's providence by fire.
With spiritual food he fed his servants well,
But free from flesh that made the Jews rebel:
And Moses' laws he held in more account,
For forty days of fasting in the mount.

To speak the rest who better are forgot, 630
Would tire a well-breathed witness of the plot.
Yet Corah, thou shalt from oblivion pass;
Erect thyself, thou monumental brass,
High as the serpent of thy metal made,
While nations stand secure beneath thy shade.
What though his birth were base, yet comets rise
From earthly vapours, ere they shine in skies.
Prodigious actions may as well be done
By weaver's issue, as by prince's son.
This arch attestor for the public good 640
By that one deed ennobles all his blood.
Who ever ask'd the witness's high race,
Whose oath with martyrdom did Stephen grace?
Ours was a Levite, and as times went then,
His tribe were God Almighty's gentlemen.
Sunk were his eyes, his voice was harsh and loud,
Sure signs he neither choleric was, nor proud.
His long chin proved his wit; his saint-like grace
A church vermilion, and a Moses' face.
His memory miraculously great, 650
Could plots, exceeding man's belief, repeat;
Which therefore cannot be accounted lies,
For human wit could never such devise.
Some future truths are mingled in his book;
But where the witness fail'd, the prophet spoke.
Some things like visionary flights appear;
The spirit caught him up the Lord knows where;
And gave him his rabbinical degree,

Unknown to foreign university.
His judgment yet his memory did excel; 660
Which pieced his wondrous evidence so well,
And suited to the temper of the times,
Then groaning under Jebusitic crimes.
Let Israel's foes suspect his heavenly call,
And rashly judge his wit apocryphal;
Our laws for such affronts have forfeits made;
He takes his life who takes away his trade.
Were I myself in witness Corah's place,
The wretch who did me such a dire disgrace,
Should whet my memory, though once forgot, 670
To make him an appendix of my plot.
His zeal to heaven made him his prince despise,
And load his person with indignities.
But zeal peculiar privilege affords,
Indulging latitude to deeds and words:
And Corah might for Agag's murder call,
In terms as coarse as Samuel used to Saul.
What others in his evidence did join,
The best that could be had for love or coin,
In Corah's own predicament will fall: 680
For witness is a common name to all.
  Surrounded thus with friends of every sort,
Deluded Absalom forsakes the court:
Impatient of high hopes, urged with renown,
And fired with near possession of a crown.
The admiring crowd are dazzled with surprise,
And on his goodly person feed their eyes.

His joy conceal'd he sets himself to show;
On each side bowing popularly low:
His looks, his gestures, and his words he frames, 690
And with familiar ease repeats their names.
Thus form'd by nature, furnish'd out with arts,
He glides unfelt into their secret hearts.
Then, with a kind compassionating look,
And sighs, bespeaking pity ere he spoke,
Few words he said; but easy those and fit,
More slow than Hybla-drops, and far more sweet.

  I mourn, my countrymen, your lost estate;
Though far unable to prevent your fate:
Behold a banish'd man for your dear cause 700
Exposed a prey to arbitrary laws!
Yet oh! that I alone could be undone,
Cut off from empire, and no more a son!
Now all your liberties a spoil are made;
Egypt and Tyrus intercept your trade,
And Jebusites your sacred rites invade.
My father, whom with reverence yet I name,
Charm'd into ease, is careless of his fame;
And bribed with petty sums of foreign gold,
Is grown in Bathsheba's embraces old; 710
Exalts his enemies, his friends destroys,
And all his power against himself employs.
He gives, and let him give, my right away:
But why should he his own and yours betray?
He, only he, can make the nation bleed,
And he alone from my revenge is freed.

Take then my tears (with that he wiped his eyes),
'Tis all the aid my present power supplies:
No court-informer can these arms accuse;
These arms may sons against their fathers use: 720
And 'tis my wish, the next successor's reign,
May make no other Israelite complain.
  Youth, beauty, graceful action seldom fail;
But common interest always will prevail:
And pity never ceases to be shown
To him who makes the people's wrongs his own.
The crowd, that still believe their kings oppress,
With lifted hands their young Messiah bless:
Who now begins his progress to ordain
With chariots, horsemen, and a numerous train: 730
From east to west his glories he displays,
And, like the sun, the promised land surveys.
Fame runs before him as the morning-star,
And shouts of joy salute him from afar:
Each house receives him as a guardian god,
And consecrates the place of his abode.
But hospitable treats did most commend
Wise Issachar, his wealthy western friend.
This moving court, that caught the people's eyes,
And seem'd but pomp, did other ends disguise: 740
Achitophel had form'd it, with intent
To sound the depths, and fathom where it went,
The people's hearts, distinguish friends from foes,
And try their strength, before they came to blows.
Yet all was colour'd with a smooth pretence

Of specious love, and duty to their prince.
Religion, and redress of grievances,
Two names that always cheat, and always please,
Are often urged; and good king David's life
Endanger'd by a brother and a wife. 750
Thus in a pageant show a plot is made;
And peace itself is war in masquerade.
O foolish Israel! never warn'd by ill!
Still the same bait, and circumvented still!
Did ever men forsake their present ease,
In midst of health imagine a disease;
Take pains contingent mischiefs to foresee,
Make heirs for monarchs, and for God decree?
What shall we think? Can people give away,
Both for themselves and sons, their native sway? 760
Then they are left defenceless to the sword
Of each unbounded, arbitrary lord:
And laws are vain, by which we right enjoy,
If kings unquestion'd can those laws destroy.
Yet if the crowd be judge of fit and just,
And kings are only officers in trust,
Then this resuming covenant was declared
When kings were made, or is for ever barr'd.
If those who gave the sceptre could not tie,
By their own deed, their own posterity, 770
How then could Adam bind his future race?
How could his forfeit on mankind take place?
Or how could heavenly justice damn us all,
Who ne'er consented to our father's fall?

Then kings are slaves to those whom they command,
And tenants to their people's pleasure stand.
Add, that the power for property allow'd
Is mischievously seated in the crowd;
For who can be secure of private right,
If sovereign sway may be dissolved by might? 780
Nor is the people's judgment always true:
The most may err as grossly as the few?
And faultless kings run down by common cry,
For vice, oppression, and for tyranny.
What standard is there in a fickle rout,
Which, flowing to the mark, runs faster out?
Nor only crowds but Sanhedrims may be
Infected with this public lunacy,
And share the madness of rebellious times,
To murder monarchs for imagined crimes. 790
If they may give and take whene'er they please,
Not kings alone, the Godhead's images,
But government itself at length must fall
To nature's state, where all have right to all.
Yet, grant our lords the people kings can make,
What prudent men a settled throne would shake?
For whatsoe'er their sufferings were before,
That change they covet makes them suffer more.
All other errors but disturb a state;
But innovation is the blow of fate. 800
If ancient fabrics nod, and threat to fall,
To patch their flaws, and buttress up the wall,
Thus far 'tis duty: but here fix the mark;

For all beyond it is to touch the ark.
To change foundations, cast the frame anew,
Is work for rebels, who base ends pursue;
At once divine and human laws control,
And mend the parts by ruin of the whole,
The tampering world is subject to this curse,
To physic their disease into a worse. 810
  Now what relief can righteous David bring?
How fatal 'tis to be too good a king!
Friends he has few, so high the madness grows;
Who dare be such must be the people's foes.
Yet some there were, even in the worst of days;
Some let me name, and naming is to praise.
  In this short file Barzillai first appears;
Barzillai, crown'd with honour and with years.
Long since, the rising rebels he withstood
In regions waste beyond the Jordan's flood: 820
Unfortunately brave to buoy the state;
But sinking underneath his master's fate:
In exile with his godlike prince he mourn'd;
For him he suffer'd, and with him return'd.
The court he practised, not the courtier's art:
Large was his wealth, but larger was his heart,
Which well the noblest objects knew to choose,
The fighting warrior, and recording muse.
His bed could once a fruitful issue boast;
Now more than half a father's name is lost. 830
His eldest hope, with every grace adorn'd,
By me, so Heaven will have it, always mourn'd,

And always honour'd, snatch'd in manhood's prime
By unequal fates, and providence's crime:
Yet not before the goal of honour won,
All parts fulfill'd of subject and of son:
Swift was the race, but short the time to run.
O narrow circle, but of power divine,
Scanted in space, but perfect in thy line!
By sea, by land, thy matchless worth was known, 840
Arms thy delight, and war was all thy own:
Thy force infused the fainting Tyrians propp'd;
And haughty Pharaoh found his fortune stopp'd.
O ancient honour! O unconquer'd hand,
Whom foes unpunish'd never could withstand!
But Israel was unworthy of his name;
Short is the date of all immoderate fame.
It looks as Heaven our ruin had design'd,
And durst not trust thy fortune and thy mind.
Now, free from earth, thy disencumber'd soul 850
Mounts up, and leaves behind the clouds and starry pole:
From thence thy kindred legions mayst thou bring,
To aid the guardian angel of thy king.
  Here stop, my muse, here cease thy painful flight:
No pinions can pursue immortal height:
Tell good Barzillai thou canst sing no more,
And tell thy soul she should have fled before:
Or fled she with his life, and left this verse
To hang on her departed patron's hearse?
Now take thy steepy flight from heaven, and see 860
If thou canst find on earth another he:

Another he would be too hard to find;
See then whom thou canst see not far behind.
Zadoc the priest, whom, shunning power and place,
His lowly mind advanced to David's grace.
With him the Sagan of Jerusalem,
Of hospitable soul, and noble stem;
Him* of the western dome, whose weighty sense
Flows in fit words and heavenly eloquence.
The prophets' sons, by such example led, 870
To learning and to loyalty were bred:
For colleges on bounteous kings depend,
And never rebel was to arts a friend.
To these succeed the pillars of the laws,
Who best can plead, and best can judge a cause.
Next them a train of loyal peers ascend;
Sharp-judging Adriel, the Muses' friend,
Himself a Muse: in Sanhedrim's debate
True to his prince, but not a slave of state:
Whom David's love with honours did adorn, 880
That from his disobedient son were torn.
Jotham, of piercing wit, and pregnant thought;
Endued by nature, and by learning taught
To move assemblies, who but only tried
The worse awhile, then chose the better side:
Nor chose alone, but turn'd the balance too, —
So much the weight of one brave man can do.
Hushai, the friend of David in distress;
In public storms of manly steadfastness:

---

* 'Him:' Dr Dolben, Bishop of Rochester.

By foreign treaties he inform'd his youth, 890
And join'd experience to his native truth.
His frugal care supplied the wanting throne —
Frugal for that, but bounteous of his own:
'Tis easy conduct when exchequers flow;
But hard the task to manage well the low;
For sovereign power is too depress'd or high,
When kings are forced to sell, or crowds to buy.
Indulge one labour more, my weary muse,
For Amiel: who can Amiel's praise refuse?
Of ancient race by birth, but nobler yet 900
In his own worth, and without title great:
The Sanhedrim long time as chief he ruled,
Their reason guided, and their passion cool'd:
So dexterous was he in the crown's defence,
So form'd to speak a loyal nation's sense,
That, as their band was Israel's tribes in small,
So fit was he to represent them all.
Now rasher charioteers the seat ascend,
Whose loose careers his steady skill commend:
They, like the unequal ruler of the day,* 910
Misguide the seasons, and mistake the way;
While he withdrawn, at their mad labours smiles,
And safe enjoys the sabbath of his toils.
  These were the chief, a small but faithful band
Of worthies, in the breach who dared to stand,
And tempt the united fury of the land:
With grief they view'd such powerful engines bent,

---

* 'Ruler of the day:' Phaeton.

To batter down the lawful government.
A numerous faction, with pretended frights,
In Sanhedrims to plume the regal rights; 920
The true successor from the court removed;
The plot, by hireling witnesses, improved.
These ills they saw, and, as their duty bound,
They show'd the King the danger of the wound;
That no concessions from the throne would please,
But lenitives fomented the disease:
That Absalom, ambitious of the crown,
Was made the lure to draw the people down:
That false Achitophel's pernicious hate
Had turn'd the Plot to ruin church and state: 930
The council violent, the rabble worse:
That Shimei taught Jerusalem to curse.
 With all these loads of injuries oppress'd,
And long revolving in his careful breast
The event of things, at last his patience tired,
Thus, from his royal throne, by Heaven inspired,
The god-like David spoke; with awful fear,
His train their Maker in their master hear.
 Thus long have I, by native mercy sway'd,
My wrongs dissembled, my revenge delay'd: 940
So willing to forgive the offending age;
So much the father did the king assuage.
But now so far my clemency they slight,
The offenders question my forgiving right:
That one was made for many, they contend;
But 'tis to rule; for that's a monarch's end.

They call my tenderness of blood, my fear:
Though manly tempers can the longest bear.
Yet, since they will divert my native course,
'Tis time to show I am not good by force. 950
Those heap'd affronts that haughty subjects bring,
Are burdens for a camel, not a king.
Kings are the public pillars of the state,
Born to sustain and prop the nation's weight:
If my young Samson will pretend a call
To shake the column, let him share the fall:
But oh, that yet he would repent and live!
How easy 'tis for parents to forgive!
With how few tears a pardon might be won
From nature, pleading for a darling son! 960
Poor, pitied youth, by my paternal care,
Raised up to all the height his frame could bear!
Had God ordain'd his fate for empire born,
He would have given his soul another turn:
Gull'd with a patriot's name, whose modern sense
Is one that would by law supplant his prince;
The people's brave, the politician's tool;
Never was patriot yet, but was a fool.
Whence comes it, that religion and the laws
Should more be Absalom's than David's cause? 970
His old instructor, ere he lost his place,
Was never thought endued with so much grace.
Good heavens, how faction can a patriot paint!
My rebel ever proves my people's saint.
Would they impose an heir upon the throne,

Let Sanhedrims be taught to give their own.
A king's at least a part of government;
And mine as requisite as their consent:
Without my leave a future king to choose,
Infers a right the present to depose. 980
True, they petition me to approve their choice:
But Esau's hands suit ill with Jacob's voice.
My pious subjects for my safety pray,
Which to secure, they take my power away.
From plots and treasons Heaven preserve my years,
But save me most from my petitioners!
Insatiate as the barren womb or grave,
God cannot grant so much as they can crave.
What then is left, but with a jealous eye
To guard the small remains of royalty? 990
The law shall still direct my peaceful sway,
And the same law teach rebels to obey:
Votes shall no more establish'd power control,
Such votes as make a part exceed the whole.
No groundless clamours shall my friends remove,
Nor crowds have power to punish ere they prove;
For gods and god-like kings their care express,
Still to defend their servants in distress.
O that my power to saving were confined!
Why am I forced, like Heaven, against my mind; 1000
To make examples of another kind?
Must I at length the sword of justice draw?
Oh, cursed effects of necessary law!
How ill my fear they by my mercy scan!

Beware the fury of a patient man!
Law they require, let law then show her face;
They could not be content to look on grace,
Her hinder parts, but with a daring eye
To tempt the terror of her front and die.
By their own arts 'tis righteously decreed, 1010
Those dire artificers of death shall bleed.
Against themselves their witnesses will swear,
Till, viper-like, their mother-plot they tear;
And suck for nutriment that bloody gore,
Which was their principle of life before.
Their Belial with their Beelzebub will fight:
Thus on my foes, my foes shall do me right.
Nor doubt the event: for factious crowds engage,
In their first onset, all their brutal rage.
Then let them take an unresisted course; 1020
Retire, and traverse, and delude their force;
But when they stand all breathless, urge the fight,
And rise upon them with redoubled might —
For lawful power is still superior found;
When long driven back, at length it stands the ground.
 He said: The Almighty, nodding, gave consent;
And peals of thunder shook the firmament.
Henceforth a series of new time began,
The mighty years in long procession ran:
Once more the god-like David was restored, 1030
And willing nations knew their lawful lord.

PART II.

"Si quis tamen haec quoque, si quis captus amore leget."

TO THE READER.

In the year 1680, Mr Dryden undertook the poem of Absalom and Achitophel, upon the desire of King Charles the Second. The performance was applauded by every one; and several persons pressing him to write a second part, he, upon declining it himself, spoke to Mr Tate[*] to write one, and gave him his advice in the direction of it; and that part beginning with

"Next these, a troop of busy spirits press,"

and ending with

"To talk like Doeg, and to write like thee,"

containing near two hundred verses, mere entirely Mr Dryden's composition, besides some touches in other places.

DERRICK.

---

[*] The second part was written by Mr Nahum Tate, and is by no means equal to the first, though Dryden corrected it throughout. The poem is here printed complete.

Since men like beasts each other's prey were made,
Since trade began, and priesthood grew a trade,
Since realms were form'd, none sure so cursed as those
That madly their own happiness oppose;
There Heaven itself and god-like kings, in vain
Shower down the manna of a gentle reign;
While pamper'd crowds to mad sedition run,
And monarchs by indulgence are undone.
Thus David's clemency was fatal grown,
While wealthy faction awed the wanting throne. 10
For now their sovereign's orders to contemn
Was held the charter of Jerusalem;
His rights to invade, his tributes to refuse,
A privilege peculiar to the Jews;
As if from heavenly call this licence fell,
And Jacob's seed were chosen to rebel!
 Achitophel with triumph sees his crimes
Thus suited to the madness of the times;
And Absalom, to make his hopes succeed,
Of flattering charms no longer stands in need; 20
While fond of change, though ne'er so dearly bought,
Our tribes outstrip the youth's ambitious thought;
His swiftest hopes with swifter homage meet,
And crowd their servile necks beneath his feet.
Thus to his aid while pressing tides repair,
He mounts and spreads his streamers in the air.
The charms of empire might his youth mislead,
But what can our besotted Israel plead?
Sway'd by a monarch, whose serene command

Seems half the blessing of our promised land: 30
Whose only grievance is excess of ease;
Freedom our pain, and plenty our disease!
Yet, as all folly would lay claim to sense,
And wickedness ne'er wanted a pretence,
With arguments they'd make their treason good,
And righteous David's self with slanders load:
That arts of foreign sway he did affect,
And guilty Jebusites from law protect,
Whose very chiefs, convict, were never freed,
Nay, we have seen their sacrificers bleed! 40
Accusers' infamy is urged in vain,
While in the bounds of sense they did contain;
But soon they launch into the unfathom'd tide,
And in the depths they knew disdain'd to ride.
For probable discoveries to dispense,
Was thought below a pension'd evidence;
Mere truth was dull, nor suited with the port
Of pamper'd Corah when advanced to court.
No less than wonders now they will impose,
And projects void of grace or sense disclose. 50
Such was the charge on pious Michal brought, —
Michal that ne'er was cruel, even in thought, —
The best of queens, and most obedient wife,
Impeach'd of cursed designs on David's life!
His life, the theme of her eternal prayer,
'Tis scarce so much his guardian angel's care.
Not summer morns such mildness can disclose,
The Hermon lily, nor the Sharon rose.

Neglecting each vain pomp of majesty,
Transported Michal feeds her thoughts on high. 60
She lives with angels, and, as angels do,
Quits heaven sometimes to bless the world below;
Where, cherish'd by her bounties' plenteous spring,
Reviving widows smile, and orphans sing.
Oh! when rebellious Israel's crimes at height,
Are threaten'd with her Lord's approaching fate,
The piety of Michal then remain
In Heaven's remembrance, and prolong his reign!
 Less desolation did the pest pursue,
That from Dan's limits to Beersheba flew; 70
Less fatal the repeated wars of Tyre,
And less Jerusalem's avenging fire.
With gentler terror these our state o'erran,
Than since our evidencing days began!
On every cheek a pale confusion sate,
Continued fear beyond the worst of fate!
Trust was no more; art, science useless made;
All occupations lost but Corah's trade.
Meanwhile a guard on modest Corah wait,
If not for safety, needful yet for state. 80
Well might he deem each peer and prince his slave,
And lord it o'er the tribes which he could save:
Even vice in him was virtue — what sad fate,
But for his honesty had seized our state!
And with what tyranny had we been cursed,
Had Corah never proved a villain first!
To have told his knowledge of the intrigue in gross,

Had been, alas! to our deponent's loss:
The travell'd Levite had the experience got,
To husband well, and make the best of's Plot; 90
And therefore, like an evidence of skill,
With wise reserves secured his pension still;
Nor quite of future power himself bereft,
But limbos large for unbelievers left.
And now his writ such reverence had got,
'Twas worse than plotting to suspect his Plot.
Some were so well convinced, they made no doubt
Themselves to help the founder'd swearers out.
Some had their sense imposed on by their fear,
But more for interest sake believe and swear: 100
Even to that height with some the frenzy grew,
They raged to find their danger not prove true.
  Yet, than all these a viler crew remain,
Who with Achitophel the cry maintain;
Not urged by fear, nor through misguided sense, —
Blind zeal and starving need had some pretence;
But for the good old cause, that did excite
The original rebels' wiles — revenge and spite.
These raise the plot, to have the scandal thrown
Upon the bright successor of the crown, 110
Whose virtue with such wrongs they had pursued,
As seem'd all hope of pardon to exclude.
Thus, while on private ends their zeal is built,
The cheated crowd applaud, and share their guilt.
  Such practices as these, too gross to lie
Long unobserved by each discerning eye,

The more judicious Israelites unspell'd,
Though still the charm the giddy rabble held.
Even Absalom, amidst the dazzling beams
Of empire, and ambition's flattering dreams, 120
Perceives the plot, too foul to be excused,
To aid designs, no less pernicious, used.
And, filial sense yet striving in his breast,
Thus to Achitophel his doubts express'd:
  Why are my thoughts upon a crown employ'd.
Which, once obtain'd, can be but half enjoy'd?
Not so when virtue did my arms require,
And to my father's wars I flew entire.
My regal power how will my foes resent,
When I myself have scarce my own consent! 130
Give me a son's unblemish'd truth again,
Or quench the sparks of duty that remain.
How slight to force a throne that legions guard
The task to me! to prove unjust, how hard!
And if the imagined guilt thus wound my thought,
What will it when the tragic scene is wrought!
Dire war must first be conjured from below,
The realm we rule we first must overthrow;
And, when the civil furies are on wing,
That blind and undistinguish'd slaughters fling, 140
Who knows what impious chance may reach the king?
Oh, rather let me perish in the strife,
Than have my crown the price of David's life!
Or if the tempest of the war he stand,
In peace, some vile officious villain's hand

His soul's anointed temple may invade;
Or, press'd by clamorous crowds, myself be made
His murderer; rebellious crowds, whose guilt
Shall dread his vengeance till his blood be spilt.
Which, if my filial tenderness oppose, 150
Since to the empire by their arms I rose,
Those very arms on me shall be employ'd,
A new usurper crown'd, and I destroy'd:
The same pretence of public good will hold,
And new Achitophels be found as bold
To urge the needful change — perhaps the old.
 He said. The statesman with a smile replies,
A smile that did his rising spleen disguise:
My thoughts presumed our labours at an end;
And are we still with conscience to contend? 160
Whose want in kings as needful is allow'd,
As 'tis for them to find it in the crowd.
Far in the doubtful passage you are gone,
And only can be safe by pressing on.
The crown's true heir, a prince severe and wise,
Has view'd your motions long with jealous eyes,
Your person's charms, your more prevailing arts,
And mark'd your progress in the people's hearts,
Whose patience is the effect of stinted power,
But treasures vengeance for the fatal hour; 170
And if remote the peril he can bring,
Your present danger's greater from the king.
Let not a parent's name deceive your sense,
Nor trust the father in a jealous prince!

Your trivial faults if he could so resent,
To doom you little less than banishment,
What rage must your presumption since inspire!
Against his orders you return from Tyre.
Nor only so, but with a pomp more high,
And open court of popularity, 180
The factious tribes. — And this reproof from thee!
The prince replies; Oh, statesman's winding skill,
They first condemn that first advised the ill!
 Illustrious youth! returned Achitophel,
Misconstrue not the words that mean you well;
The course you steer I worthy blame conclude,
But 'tis because you leave it unpursued.
A monarch's crown with fate surrounded lies,
Who reach, lay hold on death that miss the prize.
Did you for this expose yourself to show, 190
And to the crowd bow popularly low?
For this your glorious progress next ordain,
With chariots, horsemen, and a numerous train?
With fame before you, like the morning star,
And shouts of joy saluting from afar?
Oh, from the heights you've reach'd but take a view,
Scarce leading Lucifer could fall like you!
And must I here my shipwreck'd arts bemoan?
Have I for this so oft made Israel groan?
Your single interest with the nation weigh'd, 200
And turn'd the scale where your desires were laid;
Even when at helm a course so dangerous moved
To land your hopes, as my removal proved. —

I not dispute, the royal youth replies,
The known perfection of your policies;
Nor in Achitophel yet grudge or blame
The privilege that statesmen ever claim;
Who private interest never yet pursued,
But still pretended 'twas for others good:
What politician yet e'er 'scaped his fate, 210
Who, saving his own neck, not saved the state?
From hence, on every humorous wind that veer'd,
With shifted sails a several course you steer'd.
What form of sway did David e'er pursue,
That seem'd like absolute, but sprung from you?
Who at your instance quash'd each penal law,
That kept dissenting factious Jews in awe;
And who suspends fix'd laws, may abrogate,
That done, form new, and so enslave the state.
Even property whose champion now you stand, 220
And seem for this the idol of the land,
Did ne'er sustain such violence before,
As when your counsel shut the royal store;
Advice, that ruin to whole tribes procured,
But secret kept till your own banks secured.
Recount with this the triple covenant broke,
And Israel fitted for a foreign yoke;
Nor here your counsel's fatal progress stay'd,
But sent our levied powers to Pharaoh's aid.
Hence Tyre and Israel, low in ruins laid, 230
And Egypt, once their scorn, their common terror made.
Even yet of such a season can we dream,

When royal rights you made your darling theme.
For power unlimited could reasons draw,
And place prerogative above the law;
Which, on your fall from office, grew unjust,
The laws made king, the king a slave in trust:
Whom with state-craft, to interest only true,
You now accuse of ills contrived by you.
 To this hell's agent: Royal youth, fix here, 240
Let interest be the star by which you steer.
Hence to repose your trust in me was wise,
Whose interest most in your advancement lies.
A tie so firm as always will avail,
When friendship, nature, and religion fail;
On ours the safety of the crowd depends;
Secure the crowd, and we obtain our ends,
Whom I will cause so far our guilt to share,
Till they are made our champions by their fear.
What opposition can your rival bring, 250
While Sanhedrims are jealous of the king?
His strength as yet in David's friendship lies,
And what can David's self without supplies?
Who with exclusive bills must now dispense,
Debar the heir, or starve in his defence.
Conditions which our elders ne'er will quit,
And David's justice never can admit.
Or forced by wants his brother to betray,
To your ambition next he clears the way;
For if succession once to nought they bring, 260
Their next advance removes the present king:

Persisting else his senates to dissolve,
In equal hazard shall his reign involve.
Our tribes, whom Pharaoh's power so much alarms,
Shall rise without their prince to oppose his arms;
Nor boots it on what cause at first they join,
Their troops, once up, are tools for our design.
At least such subtle covenants shall be made,
Till peace itself is war in masquerade.
Associations of mysterious sense, 270
Against, but seeming for, the king's defence:
Even on their courts of justice fetters draw,
And from our agents muzzle up their law.
By which a conquest if we fail to make,
'Tis a drawn game at worst, and we secure our stake.
 He said, and for the dire success depends
On various sects, by common guilt made friends.
Whose heads, though ne'er so differing in their creed,
I' th' point of treason yet were well agreed.
'Mongst these, extorting Ishban first appears, 280
Pursued by a meagre troop of bankrupt heirs.
Blest times when Ishban, he whose occupation
So long has been to cheat, reforms the nation!
Ishban of conscience suited to his trade,
As good a saint as usurer ever made.
Yet Mammon has not so engross'd him quite,
But Belial lays as large a claim of spite;
Who, for those pardons from his prince he draws,
Returns reproaches, and cries up the cause.
That year in which the city he did sway, 290

He left rebellion in a hopeful way,
Yet his ambition once was found so bold,
To offer talents of extorted gold;
Could David's wants have so been bribed, to shame
And scandalize our peerage with his name;
For which, his dear sedition he'd forswear,
And e'en turn loyal to be made a peer.
Next him, let railing Rabsheka have place,
So full of zeal he has no need of grace;
A saint that can both flesh and spirit use, 300
Alike haunt conventicles and the stews:
Of whom the question difficult appears,
If most i' th' preacher's or the bawd's arrears.
What caution could appear too much in him
That keeps the treasure of Jerusalem!
Let David's brother but approach the town,
Double our guards, he cries, we are undone.
Protesting that he dares not sleep in 's bed
Lest he should rise next morn without his head.
 Next* these, a troop of busy spirits press, 310
Of little fortunes, and of conscience less;
With them the tribe, whose luxury had drain'd
Their banks, in former sequestrations gain'd;
Who rich and great by past rebellions grew,
And long to fish the troubled streams anew.
Some future hopes, some present payment draws,
To sell their conscience and espouse the cause.
Such stipends those vile hirelings best befit, 318

---

* 'Next:' from this to the line, 'To talk like Doeg, and to write like thee,' is Dryden's own.

Priests without grace, and poets without wit.
Shall that false Hebronite escape our curse,
Judas, that keeps the rebels' pension-purse;
Judas, that pays the treason-writer's fee,
Judas, that well deserves his namesake's tree;
Who at Jerusalem's own gates erects
His college for a nursery of sects;
Young prophets with an early care secures,
And with the dung of his own arts manures!
What have the men of Hebron here to do?
What part in Israel's promised land have you?
Here Phaleg the lay-Hebronite is come, 330
'Cause like the rest he could not live at home;
Who from his own possessions could not drain
An omer even of Hebronitish grain;
Here struts it like a patriot, and talks high
Of injured subjects, alter'd property:
An emblem of that buzzing insect just,
That mounts the wheel, and thinks she raises dust.
Can dry bones live? or skeletons produce
The vital warmth of cuckoldising juice?
Slim Phaleg could, and at the table fed, 340
Return'd the grateful product to the bed.
A waiting-man to travelling nobles chose,
He his own laws would saucily impose,
Till bastinadoed back again he went,
To learn those manners he to teach was sent.
Chastised he ought to have retreated home,
But he reads politics to Absalom.

For never Hebronite, though kick'd and scorn'd,
To his own country willingly return'd.
— But leaving famish'd Phaleg to be fed, 350
And to talk treason for his daily bread,
Let Hebron, nay let hell, produce a man
So made for mischief as Ben–Jochanan.
A Jew of humble parentage was he,
By trade a Levite, though of low degree:
His pride no higher than the desk aspired,
But for the drudgery of priests was hired
To read and pray in linen ephod brave,
And pick up single shekels from the grave.
Married at last, but finding charge come faster, 360
He could not live by God, but changed his master:
Inspired by want, was made a factious tool,
They got a villain, and we lost a fool.
Still violent, whatever cause he took,
But most against the party he forsook;
For renegadoes, who ne'er turn by halves,
Are bound in conscience to be double knaves.
So this prose-prophet took most monstrous pains
To let his masters see he earn'd his gains.
But, as the devil owes all his imps a shame, 370
He chose the apostate for his proper theme;
With little pains he made the picture true,
And from reflection took the rogue he drew.
A wondrous work, to prove the Jewish nation
In every age a murmuring generation;
To trace them from their infancy of sinning,

And show them factious from their first beginning.
To prove they could rebel, and rail, and mock,
Much to the credit of the chosen flock;
A strong authority which must convince, 380
That saints own no allegiance to their prince;
As 'tis a leading-card to make a whore,
To prove her mother had turn'd up before.
But, tell me, did the drunken patriarch bless
The son that show'd his father's nakedness?
Such thanks the present church thy pen will give,
Which proves rebellion was so primitive.
Must ancient failings be examples made?
Then murderers from Cain may learn their trade.
As thou the heathen and the saint hast drawn, 390
Methinks the apostate was the better man:
And thy hot father, waving my respect,
Not of a mother-church but of a sect.
And such he needs must be of thy inditing;
This comes of drinking asses' milk and writing.
If Balak should be call'd to leave his place,
As profit is the loudest call of grace,
His temple, dispossess'd of one, would be
Replenished with seven devils more by thee.
  Levi, thou art a load, I'll lay thee down, 400
And show Rebellion bare, without a gown;
Poor slaves in metre, dull and addle-pated,
Who rhyme below even David's psalms translated;
Some in my speedy pace I must outrun,
As lame Mephibosheth the wizard's son:

To make quick way I'll leap o'er heavy blocks,
Shun rotten Uzza, as I would the pox;
And hasten Og and Doeg to rehearse,
Two fools that crutch their feeble sense on verse:
Who, by my muse, to all succeeding times 410
Shall live in spite of their own doggrel rhymes.
 Doeg, though without knowing how or why,
Made still a blundering kind of melody;
Spurr'd boldly on, and dash'd through thick and thin,
Through sense and nonsense, never out nor in;
Free from all meaning, whether good or bad,
And, in one word, heroically mad:
He was too warm on picking-work to dwell,
But fagoted his notions as they fell,
And if they rhymed and rattled, all was well. 420
Spiteful he is not, though he wrote a satire,
For still there goes some thinking to ill-nature:
He needs no more than birds and beasts to think,
All his occasions are to eat and drink.
If he call rogue and rascal from a garret,
He means you no more mischief than a parrot;
The words for friend and foe alike were made,
To fetter them in verse is all his trade.
For almonds he'll cry whore to his own mother:
And call young Absalom king David's brother. 430
Let him be gallows-free by my consent,
And nothing suffer, since he nothing meant.
Hanging supposes human soul and reason —
This animal's below committing treason:

Shall he be hang'd who never could rebel?
That's a preferment for Achitophel.
The woman. . . . . . .
Was rightly sentenced by the law to die;
But 'twas hard fate that to the gallows led
The dog that never heard the statute read. 440
Railing in other men may be a crime,
But ought to pass for mere instinct in him:
Instinct he follows, and no further knows,
For to write verse with him is to transpose.
'Twere pity treason at his door to lay,
Who makes heaven's gate a lock to its own key:[*]
Let him rail on, let his invective muse
Have four and twenty letters to abuse,
Which, if he jumbles to one line of sense,
Indict him of a capital offence. 450
In fireworks give him leave to vent his spite —
Those are the only serpents he can write;
The height of his ambition is, we know,
But to be master of a puppet-show;
On that one stage his works may yet appear,
And a month's harvest keeps him all the year.
 Now stop your noses, readers, all and some,
For here's a tun of midnight work to come;
Og, from a treason-tavern rolling home,
Round as a globe, and liquor'd every chink, 460
Goodly and great he sails behind his link;
With all this bulk there's nothing lost in Og,

---

[*] 'Who makes,' &c.: a line quoted from Settle.

For every inch that is not fool is rogue:
A monstrous mass of foul corrupted matter,
As all the devils had spued to make the batter.
When wine has given him courage to blaspheme,
He curses God, but God before cursed him;
And if man could have reason, none has more,
That made his paunch so rich, and him so poor.
With wealth he was not trusted, for Heaven knew 470
What 'twas of old to pamper up a Jew;
To what would he on quail and pheasant swell,
That even on tripe and carrion could rebel?
But though Heaven made him poor (with reverence speaking),
He never was a poet of God's making;
The midwife laid her hand on his thick skull,
With this prophetic blessing — Be thou dull;
Drink, swear, and roar, forbear no lewd delight
Fit for thy bulk — do anything but write:
Thou art of lasting make, like thoughtless men, 480
A strong nativity — but for the pen!
Eat opium, mingle arsenic in thy drink,
Still thou mayst live, avoiding pen and ink.
I see, I see, 'tis counsel given in vain,
For treason botch'd in rhyme will be thy bane;
Rhyme is the rock on which thou art to wreck,
'Tis fatal to thy fame and to thy neck:
Why should thy metre good king David blast?
A psalm of his will surely be thy last.
Dar'st thou presume in verse to meet thy foes, 490
Thou whom the penny pamphlet foil'd in prose?

Doeg, whom God for mankind's mirth has made,
O'ertops thy talent in thy very trade;
Doeg to thee, thy paintings are so coarse,
A poet is, though he's the poet's horse.
A double noose thou on thy neck dost pull,
For writing treason, and for writing dull;
To die for faction is a common evil,
But to be hang'd for nonsense is the devil:
Hadst thou the glories of thy king express'd, 500
Thy praises had been satire at the best;
But thou in clumsy verse, unlick'd, unpointed,
Hast shamefully defied the Lord's anointed:
I will not rake the dunghill for thy crimes,
For who would read thy life that reads thy rhymes?
But of king David's foes, be this the doom,
May all be like the young man Absalom;
And, for my foes, may this their blessing be,
To talk like Doeg, and to write like thee!
 Achitophel, each rank, degree, and age, 510
For various ends neglects not to engage;
The wise and rich, for purse and counsel brought,
The fools and beggars, for their number sought:
Who yet not only on the town depends,
For even in court the faction had its friends;
These thought the places they possess'd too small,
And in their hearts wish'd court and king to fall:
Whose names the muse disdaining, holds i' the dark,
Thrust in the villain herd without a mark;
With parasites and libel-spawning imps, 520

Intriguing fops, dull jesters, and worse pimps.
Disdain the rascal rabble to pursue,
Their set cabals are yet a viler crew:
See where, involved in common smoke, they sit;
Some for our mirth, some for our satire fit:
These, gloomy, thoughtful, and on mischief bent,
While those, for mere good-fellowship, frequent
The appointed club, can let sedition pass,
Sense, nonsense, anything to employ the glass;
And who believe, in their dull honest hearts, 530
The rest talk reason but to show their parts;
Who ne'er had wit or will for mischief yet,
But pleased to be reputed of a set.
 But in the sacred annals of our plot,
Industrious Arod never be forgot:
The labours of this midnight-magistrate,
May vie with Corah's to preserve the state.
In search of arms, he fail'd not to lay hold
On war's most powerful, dangerous weapon — gold.
And last, to take from Jebusites all odds, 540
Their altars pillaged, stole their very gods;
Oft would he cry, when treasure he surprised,
'Tis Baalish gold in David's coin disguised;
Which to his house with richer relics came,
While lumber idols only fed the flame:
For our wise rabble ne'er took pains to inquire,
What 'twas he burnt, so 't made a rousing fire.
With which our elder was enrich'd no more
Than false Gehazi with the Syrian's store;

So poor, that when our choosing-tribes were met, 550
Even for his stinking votes he ran in debt;
For meat the wicked, and, as authors think,
The saints he choused for his electing drink;
Thus every shift and subtle method past,
And all to be no Zaken at the last.
 Now, raised on Tyre's sad ruins, Pharaoh's pride
Soar'd high, his legions threatening far and wide;
As when a battering storm engender'd high,
By winds upheld, hangs hovering in the sky,
Is gazed upon by every trembling swain — 560
This for his vineyard fears, and that, his grain;
For blooming plants, and flowers new opening these,
For lambs yean'd lately, and far-labouring bees:
To guard his stock each to the gods does call,
Uncertain where the fire-charged clouds will fall:
Even so the doubtful nations watch his arms,
With terror each expecting his alarms.
Where, Judah! where was now thy lion's roar?
Thou only couldst the captive lands restore;
But thou, with inbred broils and faction press'd, 570
From Egypt needst a guardian with the rest.
Thy prince from Sanhedrims no trust allow'd,
Too much the representers of the crowd,
Who for their own defence give no supply,
But what the crown's prerogatives must buy:
As if their monarch's rights to violate
More needful were, than to preserve the state!
From present dangers they divert their care,

And all their fears are of the royal heir;
Whom now the reigning malice of his foes 580
Unjudged would sentence, and e'er crown'd depose.
Religion the pretence, but their decree
To bar his reign, whate'er his faith shall be!
By Sanhedrims and clamorous crowds thus press'd,
What passions rent the righteous David's breast!
Who knows not how to oppose or to comply —
Unjust to grant, or dangerous to deny!
How near, in this dark juncture, Israel's fate,
Whose peace one sole expedient could create,
Which yet the extremest virtue did require, 590
Even of that prince whose downfall they conspire!
His absence David does with tears advise,
To appease their rage. Undaunted he complies.
Thus he, who, prodigal of blood and ease,
A royal life exposed to winds and seas,
At once contending with the waves and fire,
And heading danger in the wars of Tyre,
Inglorious now forsakes his native sand,
And like an exile quits the promised land!
Our monarch scarce from pressing tears refrains, 600
And painfully his royal state maintains,
Who now, embracing on the extremest shore,
Almost revokes what he enjoin'd before:
Concludes at last more trust to be allow'd
To storms and seas than to the raging crowd!
Forbear, rash muse! the parting scene to draw,
With silence charm'd as deep as theirs that saw!

Not only our attending nobles weep,
But hardy sailors swell with tears the deep!
The tide restrain'd her course, and more amazed, 610
The twin-stars on the royal brothers gazed:
While this sole fear —
Does trouble to our suffering hero bring,
Lest next the popular rage oppress the king!
Thus parting, each for the other's danger grieved,
The shore the king, and seas the prince received.
Go, injured hero! while propitious gales,
Soft as thy consort's breath, inspire thy sails;
Well may she trust her beauties on a flood,
Where thy triumphant fleets so oft have rode! 620
Safe on thy breast reclined, her rest be deep,
Rock'd like a Nereid by the waves asleep;
While happiest dreams her fancy entertain,
And to Elysian fields convert the main!
Go, injured hero! while the shores of Tyre
At thy approach so silent shall admire,
Who on thy thunder still their thoughts employ,
And greet thy landing with a trembling joy!
 On heroes thus the prophet's fate is thrown,
Admired by every nation but their own; 630
Yet while our factious Jews his worth deny,
Their aching conscience gives their tongue the lie.
Even in the worst of men the noblest parts
Confess him, and he triumphs in their hearts,
Whom to his king the best respects commend
Of subject, soldier, kinsman, prince, and friend;

All sacred names of most divine esteem,
And to perfection all sustain'd by him;
Wise, just, and constant, courtly without art,
Swift to discern and to reward desert; 640
No hour of his in fruitless ease destroy'd,
But on the noblest subjects still employ'd:
Whose steady soul ne'er learn'd to separate
Between his monarch's interest and the state;
But heaps those blessings on the royal head,
Which he well knows must be on subjects shed.
 On what pretence could then the vulgar rage
Against his worth and native rights engage?
Religious fears their argument are made —
Religious fears his sacred rights invade! 650
Of future superstition they complain,
And Jebusitic worship in his reign:
With such alarms his foes the crowd deceive,
With dangers fright, which not themselves believe.
 Since nothing can our sacred rites remove,
Whate'er the faith of the successor prove:
Our Jews their ark shall undisturb'd retain,
At least while their religion is their gain,
Who know by old experience Baal's commands
Not only claim'd their conscience, but their lands; 660
They grudge God's tithes, how therefore shall they yield
An idol full possession of the field?
Grant such a prince enthroned, we must confess
The people's sufferings than that monarch's less,
Who must to hard conditions still be bound,

And for his quiet with the crowd compound;
Or should his thoughts to tyranny incline,
Where are the means to compass the design?
Our crown's revenues are too short a store,
And jealous Sanhedrims would give no more. 670
 As vain our fears of Egypt's potent aid,
Not so has Pharaoh learn'd ambition's trade,
Nor ever with such measures can comply,
As shock the common rules of policy;
None dread like him the growth of Israel's king,
And he alone sufficient aids can bring;
Who knows that prince to Egypt can give law,
That on our stubborn tribes his yoke could draw:
At such profound expense he has not stood,
Nor dyed for this his hands so deep in blood; 680
Would ne'er through wrong and right his progress take,
Grudge his own rest, and keep the world awake,
To fix a lawless prince on Judah's throne,
First to invade our rights, and then his own;
His dear-gain'd conquests cheaply to despoil,
And reap the harvest of his crimes and toil.
We grant his wealth vast as our ocean's sand,
And curse its fatal influence on our land,
Which our bribed Jews so numerously partake,
That even an host his pensioners would make. 690
From these deceivers our divisions spring,
Our weakness, and the growth of Egypt's king;
These, with pretended friendship to the state,
Our crowds' suspicion of their prince create;

Both pleased and frighten'd with the specious cry,
To guard their sacred rites and property.
To ruin thus the chosen flock are sold,
While wolves are ta'en for guardians of the fold;
Seduced by these, we groundlessly complain,
And loathe the manna of a gentle reign: 700
Thus our forefathers' crooked paths are trod —
We trust our prince no more than they their God.
But all in vain our reasoning prophets preach,
To those whom sad experience ne'er could teach,
Who can commence new broils in bleeding scars,
And fresh remembrance of intestine wars;
When the same household mortal foes did yield,
And brothers stain'd with brothers' blood the field;
When sons' cursed steel the fathers' gore did stain,
And mothers mourn'd for sons by fathers slain! 710
When thick as Egypt's locusts on the sand,
Our tribes lay slaughter'd through the promised land,
Whose few survivors with worse fate remain,
To drag the bondage of a tyrant's reign:
Which scene of woes, unknowing we renew,
And madly, even those ills we fear, pursue;
While Pharaoh laughs at our domestic broils,
And safely crowds his tents with nations' spoils.
Yet our fierce Sanhedrim, in restless rage,
Against our absent hero still engage, 720
And chiefly urge, such did their frenzy prove,
The only suit their prince forbids to move,
Which, till obtain'd, they cease affairs of state,

And real dangers waive for groundless hate.
Long David's patience waits relief to bring,
With all the indulgence of a lawful king,
Expecting still the troubled waves would cease,
But found the raging billows still increase.
The crowd, whose insolence forbearance swells,
While he forgives too far, almost rebels. 730
At last his deep resentments silence broke,
The imperial palace shook, while thus he spoke —
   Then Justice wait, and Rigour take her time,
For lo! our mercy is become our crime:
While halting Punishment her stroke delays,
Our sovereign right, Heaven's sacred trust, decays!
For whose support even subjects' interest calls,
Woe to that kingdom where the monarch falls!
That prince who yields the least of regal sway,
So far his people's freedom does betray. 740
Right lives by law, and law subsists by power;
Disarm the shepherd, wolves the flock devour.
Hard lot of empire o'er a stubborn race,
Which Heaven itself in vain has tried with grace!
When will our reason's long-charm'd eyes unclose,
And Israel judge between her friends and foes?
When shall we see expired deceivers' sway,
And credit what our God and monarchs say?
Dissembled patriots, bribed with Egypt's gold,
Even Sanhedrims in blind obedience hold; 750
Those patriots falsehood in their actions see,
And judge by the pernicious fruit the tree.

If aught for which so loudly they declaim,
Religion, laws, and freedom, were their aim,
Our senates in due methods they had led,
To avoid those mischiefs which they seem'd to dread:
But first, e'er yet they propp'd the sinking state,
To impeach and charge, as urged by private hate,
Proves that they ne'er believed the fears they press'd,
But barbarously destroy'd the nation's rest! 760
Oh! whither will ungovern'd senates drive,
And to what bounds licentious votes arrive?
When their injustice we are press'd to share,
The monarch urged to exclude the lawful heir;
Are princes thus distinguish'd from the crowd,
And this the privilege of royal blood?
But grant we should confirm the wrongs they press,
His sufferings yet were than the people's less;
Condemn'd for life the murdering sword to wield,
And on their heirs entail a bloody field. 770
Thus madly their own freedom they betray,
And for the oppression which they fear make way;
Succession fix'd by Heaven, the kingdom's bar,
Which once dissolved, admits the flood of war;
Waste, rapine, spoil, without the assault begin,
And our mad tribes supplant the fence within.
Since then their good they will not understand,
'Tis time to take the monarch's power in hand;
Authority and force to join with skill,
And save the lunatics against their will. 780
The same rough means that 'suage the crowd, appease

Our senates raging with the crowd's disease.
Henceforth unbiass'd measures let them draw
From no false gloss, but genuine text of law;
Nor urge those crimes upon religion's score,
Themselves so much in Jebusites abhor.
Whom laws convict, and only they, shall bleed,
Nor pharisees by pharisees be freed.
Impartial justice from our throne shall shower,
All shall have right, and we our sovereign power. 790
 He said, the attendants heard with awful joy,
And glad presages their fix'd thoughts employ;
From Hebron now the suffering heir return'd,
A realm that long with civil discord mourn'd;
Till his approach, like some arriving God,
Composed and heal'd the place of his abode;
The deluge check'd that to Judea spread,
And stopp'd sedition at the fountain's head.
Thus, in forgiving, David's paths he drives,
And, chased from Israel, Israel's peace contrives. 800
The field confess'd his power in arms before,
And seas proclaim'd his triumphs to the shore;
As nobly has his sway in Hebron shown,
How fit to inherit godlike David's throne.
Through Sion's streets his glad arrival's spread,
And conscious faction shrinks her snaky head;
His train their sufferings think o'erpaid to see
The crowd's applause with virtue once agree.
Success charms all, but zeal for worth distress'd,
A virtue proper to the brave and best; 810

'Mongst whom was Jothran — Jothran always bent
To serve the crown, and loyal by descent;
Whose constancy so firm, and conduct just,
Deserved at once two royal masters' trust;
Who Tyre's proud arms had manfully withstood
On seas, and gather'd laurels from the flood;
Of learning yet no portion was denied,
Friend to the Muses and the Muses' pride.
Nor can Benaiah's worth forgotten lie,
Of steady soul when public storms were high; 820
Whose conduct, while the Moor fierce onsets made,
Secured at once our honour and our trade.
Such were the chiefs who most his sufferings mourn'd,
And view'd with silent joy the prince return'd;
While those that sought his absence to betray,
Press first their nauseous false respects to pay;
Him still the officious hypocrites molest,
And with malicious duty break his rest.
 While real transports thus his friends employ,
And foes are loud in their dissembled joy, 830
His triumphs, so resounded far and near,
Miss'd not his young ambitious rival's ear;
And as when joyful hunters' clamorous train,
Some slumbering lion wakes in Moab's plain,
Who oft had forced the bold assailants yield,
And scatter'd his pursuers through the field,
Disdaining, furls his mane and tears the ground,
His eyes inflaming all the desert round,
With roar of seas directs his chasers' way,

Provokes from far, and dares them to the fray: 840
Such rage storm'd now in Absalom's fierce breast,
Such indignation his fired eyes confess'd.
Where now was the instructor of his pride?
Slept the old pilot in so rough a tide,
Whose wiles had from the happy shore betray'd,
And thus on shelves the credulous youth convey'd?
In deep revolving thoughts he weighs his state,
Secure of craft, nor doubts to baffle fate;
At least, if his storm'd bark must go adrift,
To balk his charge, and for himself to shift, 850
In which his dexterous wit had oft been shown,
And in the wreck of kingdoms saved his own.
But now, with more than common danger press'd,
Of various resolutions stands possess'd,
Perceives the crowd's unstable zeal decay
Lest their recanting chief the cause betray,
Who on a father's grace his hopes may ground,
And for his pardon with their heads compound.
Him therefore, e'er his fortune slip her time.
The statesman plots to engage in some bold crime 860
Past pardon — whether to attempt his bed,
Or threat with open arms the royal head,
Or other daring method, and unjust,
That may confirm him in the people's trust.
But failing thus to ensnare him, nor secure
How long his foil'd ambition may endure,
Plots next to lay him by as past his date,
And try some new pretender's luckier fate;

Whose hopes with equal toil he would pursue,
Nor care what claimer's crown'd, except the true. 870
Wake, Absalom! approaching ruin shun,
And see, O see, for whom thou art undone!
How are thy honours and thy fame betray'd,
The property of desperate villains made!
Lost power and conscious fears their crimes create,
And guilt in them was little less than fate;
But why shouldst thou, from every grievance free,
Forsake thy vineyards for their stormy sea?
For thee did Canaan's milk and honey flow,
Love dress'd thy bowers, and laurels sought thy brow; 880
Preferment, wealth, and power thy vassals were,
And of a monarch all things but the care.
Oh! should our crimes again that curse draw down,
And rebel-arms once more attempt the crown,
Sure ruin waits unhappy Absalom,
Alike by conquest or defeat undone.
Who could relentless see such youth and charms
Expire with wretched fate in impious arms?
A prince so form'd, with earth's and Heaven's applause,
To triumph o'er crown'd heads in David's cause: 890
Or grant him victor, still his hopes must fail,
Who, conquering, would not for himself prevail;
The faction whom he trusts for future sway,
Him and the public would alike betray;
Amongst themselves divide the captive state,
And found their hydra-empire in his fate!
Thus having beat the clouds with painful flight,

The pitied youth, with sceptres in his sight
(So have their cruel politics decreed),
Must by that crew, that made him guilty, bleed! 900
For, could their pride brook any prince's sway,
Whom but mild David would they choose to obey?
Who once at such a gentle reign repine,
The fall of monarchy itself design:
From hate to that their reformations spring,
And David not their grievance, but the king.
Seized now with panic fear the faction lies,
Lest this clear truth strike Absalom's charm'd eyes,
Lest he perceive, from long enchantment free,
What all beside the flatter'd youth must see: 910
But whate'er doubts his troubled bosom swell,
Fair carriage still became Achitophel,
Who now an envious festival installs,
And to survey their strength the faction calls, —
Which fraud, religious worship too must gild.
But oh! how weakly does sedition build!
For lo! the royal mandate issues forth,
Dashing at once their treason, zeal, and mirth!
So have I seen disastrous chance invade,
Where careful emmets had their forage laid, 920
Whether fierce Vulcan's rage the furzy plain
Had seized, engender'd by some careless swain;
Or swelling Neptune lawless inroads made,
And to their cell of store his flood convey'd;
The commonwealth broke up, distracted go,
And in wild haste their loaded mates o'erthrow:

Even so our scatter'd guests confusedly meet,
With boil'd, baked, roast, all justling in the street;
Dejecting all, and ruefully dismay'd,
For shekel without treat or treason paid. 930
  Sedition's dark eclipse now fainter shows,
More bright each hour the royal planet grows,
Of force the clouds of envy to disperse,
In kind conjunction of assisting stars.
Here, labouring muse! those glorious chiefs relate,
That turn'd the doubtful scale of David's fate;
The rest of that illustrious band rehearse,
Immortalized in laurell'd Asaph's verse:
Hard task! yet will not I thy flight recall,
View heaven, and then enjoy thy glorious fall. 940
  First write Bezaliel, whose illustrious name
Forestalls our praise, and gives his poet fame.
The Kenites' rocky province his command,
A barren limb of fertile Canaan's land;
Which for its generous natives yet could be
Held worthy such a president as he.
Bezaliel, with each grace and virtue fraught,
Serene his looks, serene his life and thought;
On whom so largely nature heap'd her store,
There scarce remain'd for arts to give him more! 950
To aid the crown and state his greatest zeal,
His second care that service to conceal;
Of dues observant, firm to every trust,
And to the needy always more than just;
Who truth from specious falsehood can divide,

Has all the gownsmen's skill without their pride.
Thus crown'd with worth, from heights of honour won,
Sees all his glories copied in his son,
Whose forward fame should every muse engage —
Whose youth boasts skill denied to others' age. 960
Men, manners, language, books of noblest kind,
Already are the conquest of his mind;
Whose loyalty before its date was prime,
Nor waited the dull course of rolling time:
The monster faction early he dismay'd,
And David's cause long since confess'd his aid.
  Brave Abdael o'er the prophet's school was placed —
Abdael with all his father's virtue graced;
A hero who, while stars look'd wondering down,
Without one Hebrew's blood restored the crown. 970
That praise was his; what therefore did remain
For following chiefs, but boldly to maintain
That crown restored? and in this rank of fame,
Brave Abdael with the first a place must claim.
Proceed, illustrious, happy chief! proceed,
Foreseize the garlands for thy brow decreed,
While the inspired tribe attend with noblest strain
To register the glories thou shalt gain:
For sure the dew shall Gilboa's hills forsake,
And Jordan mix his stream with Sodom's lake; 980
Or seas retired, their secret stores disclose,
And to the sun their scaly brood expose,
Or swell'd above the cliffs their billows raise,
Before the muses leave their patron's praise.

Eliab our next labour does invite,
And hard the task to do Eliab right.
Long with the royal wanderer he roved,
And firm in all the turns of fortune proved.
Such ancient service and desert so large
Well claim'd the royal household for his charge. 990
His age with only one mild heiress bless'd,
In all the bloom of smiling nature dress'd,
And bless'd again to see his flower allied
To David's stock, and made young Othniel's bride.
The bright restorer of his father's youth,
Devoted to a son's and subject's truth;
Resolved to bear that prize of duty home,
So bravely sought, while sought by Absalom.
Ah, prince! the illustrious planet of thy birth,
And thy more powerful virtue, guard thy worth! 1000
That no Achitophel thy ruin boast;
Israel too much in one such wreck has lost.
 Even envy must consent to Helon's worth,
Whose soul, though Egypt glories in his birth,
Could for our captive-ark its zeal retain.
And Pharaoh's altars in their pomp disdain:
To slight his gods was small; with nobler pride,
He all the allurements of his court defied;
Whom profit nor example could betray,
But Israel's friend, and true to David's sway. 1010
What acts of favour in his province fall
On merit he confers, and freely all.
 Our list of nobles next let Amri grace,

Whose merits claim'd the Abethdin's high place;
Who, with a loyalty that did excel,
Brought all the endowments of Achitophel.
Sincere was Amri, and not only knew,
But Israel's sanctions into practice drew;
Our laws, that did a boundless ocean seem,
Were coasted all, and fathom'd all by him. 1020
No rabbin speaks like him their mystic sense,
So just, and with such charms of eloquence:
To whom the double blessing does belong,
With Moses' inspiration, Aaron's tongue.
 Than Sheva none more loyal zeal have shown,
Wakeful as Judah's lion for the crown;
Who for that cause still combats in his age,
For which his youth with danger did engage.
In vain our factious priests the cant revive;
In vain seditious scribes with libel strive 1030
To inflame the crowd; while he with watchful eye
Observes, and shoots their treasons as they fly;
Their weekly frauds his keen replies detect;
He undeceives more fast than they infect:
So Moses, when the pest on legions prey'd,
Advanced his signal, and the plague was stay'd.
 Once more, my fainting muse! thy pinions try,
And strength's exhausted store let love supply.
What tribute, Asaph, shall we render thee?
We'll crown thee with a wreath from thy own tree! 1040
Thy laurel grove no envy's flash can blast;
The song of Asaph shall for ever last.

    With wonder late posterity shall dwell
On Absalom and false Achitophel:
Thy strains shall be our slumbering prophets' dream,
And when our Sion virgins sing their theme;
Our jubilees shall with thy verse be graced,
The song of Asaph shall for ever last.
  How fierce his satire loosed! restrain'd, how tame!
How tender of the offending young man's fame! 1050
How well his worth, and brave adventures styled,
Just to his virtues, to his error mild!
No page of thine that fears the strictest view,
But teems with just reproof, or praise as due;
Not Eden could a fairer prospect yield,
All Paradise without one barren field:
Whose wit the censure of his foes has pass'd —
The song of Asaph shall for ever last.
  What praise for such rich strains shall we allow?
What just rewards the grateful crown bestow? 1060
While bees in flowers rejoice, and flowers in dew,
While stars and fountains to their course are true;
While Judah's throne, and Sion's rock stand fast,
The song of Asaph and the fame shall last!
  Still Hebron's honour'd, happy soil retains
Our royal hero's beauteous, dear remains;
Who now sails off with winds nor wishes slack,
To bring his sufferings' bright companion back.
But e'er such transport can our sense employ,
A bitter grief must poison half our joy; 1070
Nor can our coasts restored those blessings see

Without a bribe to envious destiny!
Cursed Sodom's doom for ever fix the tide
Where by inglorious chance the valiant died!
Give not insulting Askelon to know,
Nor let Gath's daughters triumph in our woe;
No sailor with the news swell Egypt's pride,
By what inglorious fate our valiant died.
Weep, Arnon! Jordan, weep thy fountains dry!
While Sion's rock dissolves for a supply. 1080
 Calm were the elements, night's silence deep,
The waves scarce murmuring, and the winds asleep;
Yet fate for ruin takes so still an hour,
And treacherous sands the princely bark devour;
Then death unworthy seized a generous race,
To virtue's scandal, and the stars' disgrace!
Oh! had the indulgent powers vouchsafed to yield,
Instead of faithless shelves, a listed field;
A listed field of Heaven's and David's foes,
Fierce as the troops that did his youth oppose, 1090
Each life had on his slaughter'd heap retired,
Not tamely, and unconquering, thus expired:
But destiny is now their only foe,
And dying, even o'er that they triumph too;
With loud last breaths their master's 'scape applaud,
Of whom kind force could scarce the fates defraud;
Who for such followers lost, O matchless mind!
At his own safety now almost repined!
Say, royal Sir! by all your fame in arms,
Your praise in peace, and by Urania's charms, 1100

If all your sufferings past so nearly press'd,
Or pierced with half so painful grief your breast?
 Thus some diviner muse her hero forms,
Not soothed with soft delights, but toss'd in storms;
Nor stretch'd on roses in the myrtle grove,
Nor crowns his days with mirth, his nights with love,
But far removed in thundering camps is found,
His slumbers short, his bed the herbless ground.
In tasks of danger always seen the first,
Feeds from the hedge, and slakes with ice his thirst, 1110
Long must his patience strive with fortune's rage,
And long-opposing gods themselves engage;
Must see his country flame, his friends destroy'd,
Before the promised empire be enjoy'd.
Such toil of fate must build a man of fame,
And such, to Israel's crown, the godlike David came.
 What sudden beams dispel the clouds so fast,
Whose drenching rains laid all our vineyards waste?
The spring, so far behind her course delay'd,
On the instant is in all her bloom array'd; 1120
The winds breathe low, the element serene;
Yet mark what motion in the waves is seen!
Thronging and busy as Hyblaean swarms,
Or straggled soldiers summon'd to their arms,
See where the princely bark in loosest pride,
With all her guardian fleet, adorns the tide!
High on her deck the royal lovers stand,
Our crimes to pardon, e'er they touch'd our land.
Welcome to Israel and to David's breast!

Here all your toils, here all your sufferings rest. 1130
 This year did Ziloah rule Jerusalem,
And boldly all sedition's surges stem,
Howe'er encumber'd with a viler pair
Than Ziph or Shimei to assist the chair;
Yet Ziloah's loyal labours so prevail'd,
That faction at the next election fail'd,
When even the common cry did justice found,
And merit by the multitude was crown'd:
With David then was Israel's peace restored,
Crowds mourn'd their error, and obey'd their lord. 1140

A KEY TO BOTH PARTS OF ABSALOM AND ACHITOPHEL.

Aldael — General Monk, Duke of Albemarle.

Abethdin — The name given, through this poem, to a Lord-Chancellor in general.

Absalom — Duke of Monmouth, natural son of King Charles II.

Achitophel — Anthony Ashley Cooper, Earl of Shaftesbury.

Adriel — John Sheffield, Earl of Mulgrave.

Agag — Sir Edmundbury Godfrey.

Amiel — Mr Seymour, Speaker of the House of Commons.

Amri — Sir Heneage Finch, Earl of Winchelsea, and Lord Chancellor.

Annabel — Duchess of Monmouth.

Arod — Sir William Waller.

Asaph — A character drawn by Tate for Dryden, in the second part of this poem.

Balaam — Earl of Huntingdon.

Balak — Barnet.

Barzillai — Duke of Ormond.

Bathsheba — Duchess of Portsmouth.

Benaiah — General Sackville.

Ben Jochanan — Rev. Samuel Johnson.

Bezaliel — Duke of Beaufort.

Caleb — Ford, Lord Grey of Werk.

Corah — Dr Titus Oates.

David — King Charles II.
Doeg — Elkanah Settle, the city poet.
Egypt — France.
Eliab — Sir Henry Bennet, Earl of Arlington.
Ethnic-Plot — The Popish Plot.
Gath — The Land of Exile, more particularly Brussels, where King Charles II. long resided.
Hebrew Priests — The Church of England Clergy.
Hebron — Scotland.
Helon — Earl of Feversham, a Frenchman by birth, and nephew to Marshal Turenne.
Hushai — Hyde, Earl of Rochester.
Ishban — Sir Robert Clayton, Alderman, and one of the City Members.
Ishbosheth — Richard Cromwell.
Israel — England.
Issachar — Thomas Thynne, Esq., who was shot in his coach.
Jebusites — Papists.
Jerusalem — London.
Jews — English.
Jonas — Sir William Jones, a great lawyer.
Jordan — Dover.
Jotham — Saville, Marquis of Halifax.
Jothram — Lord Dartmouth.
Judas — Mr Ferguson, a canting teacher.
Mephibosheth — Pordage.
Michal — Queen Catharine.
Nadab — Lord Howard of Escrick.
Og — Shadwell.

Othniel — Henry, Duke of Grafton, natural son of King Charles II. by the Duchess of Cleveland.

Phaleg — Forbes.

Pharaoh — King of France.

Rabsheka — Sir Thomas Player, one of the City Members.

Sagan of Jerusalem — Dr Compton, Bishop of London, youngest son to the Earl of Northampton.

Sanhedrim — Parliament.

Saul — Oliver Cromwell.

Sheva — Sir Roger Lestrange.

Shimei — Slingsby Bethel, Sheriff of London in 1680.

Sion — England.

Solymaean Rout — London Rebels.

Tyre — Holland.

Uzza — Jack Hall.

Zadoc — Sancroft, Archbishop of Canterbury.

Zaken — A Member of the House of Commons.

Ziloah — Sir John Moor, Lord Mayor in 1682.

Zimri — Villiers, Duke of Buckingham.